12 Chapters of My Life

P. Wolliston

DEDICATION

I am dedicating this book to God, who has been with me throughout this entire journey. There is no intent whatsoever, to portray anyone included in this book in a bad light. My hope is to do what my family has pushed me to do, which is to be my authentic self and tell MY truth.

With all the love, here are the 12 Chapters of My Life.

P. Wolliston

CONTENTS

INTRODUCTION

Be the change you wish to see in the world.
-Gandhi

12 Chapters of My Life consists of real-life occurrences from my perspective. This is a book of self-discovery, love, loss, trauma, and self-actualization. Each chapter is a puzzle piece that gives a full picture of who I am, once connected. My hope for this book is that it provides you with the understanding that you are not alone in your feelings, experiences, successes, and failures. I am inviting you to experience my healing journey and create a space for you to do the same. In each chapter, you will notice that the chapter names correlate to the chapter number. Also, you will find a short excerpt detailing relevant context, followed by a poem, and ended with an opportunity for you to reflect. An additional blank page is provided at the end of each chapter for you to express yourself freely in doodling or creating a visual of where you are or want to be. This book can be read independently but is also great for book clubs and group discussions. As I continue on my healing journey, I pray this book will be a stepping stone for yours.

-P. Wolliston

P. Wolliston

1-THE GENESIS

Most of us grew up conditioned, raised within a household with a system of requirements and expectations. I grew up in a religious household void of "hip hop" music and anything seemingly secular. My sister and I were forbidden from watching certain cartoon shows for reasons unbeknownst to us. My mother stated that the shows Pokémon and Digimon were shorthand words for "pocket monsters" and "digital monsters", and monsters were of "the devil." I never understood my mother's rationale for her requirements and expectations. I grew up with an "Alphabet" for which I structured my life around. This alphabet's tone was not that of the sweet ABC nursery rhyme we hear in daycare. The Alphabet for my life included the pressures and requirements passed down from generation to generation. In this poem, I will be sharing what was taught to me as the "Alphabet for Life".

A- bstain from immorality
B- e all that you can be
C- hrist is always on your side
D- are not to laugh or breathe

E- xcellence is the only option
F- ailure is not perceived
G- rades are most important
H- ome is far from being your sanity

I- ndependence is not welcome
J- ail seems more comforting
K- ill yourself to live like someone else
L- augh to keep people from seeing you cry
M- ore days to show no change

N- ecessities are
O- ptional
P- eople try to choose what you need
Q- uiescence is always heard before the
R- esounding shrills of screams

S- ilent stares are asking

T- railing tears are too trying to
U- nderstand what made this mess of you

V- ision starts to blur
W- ailing sirens in the distance coming to
X- amine all the clues...and the cause of this internal death is because of
Y- ou.

Z- ion is no longer, ecstasy is through, since you made her kill herself to live and breathe like you; it is time to feel the death of her and the death of you.

Reflection

Think back to the beginning of your life. How were you raised? What "Alphabet" did your guardians "teach" you? Take a moment to settle yourself, breathe, and write down the core values that were passed down to you. Do you still agree that this is the "Alphabet for Life"? If you have children or intend to have children, what piece of your alphabet would you want to exclude from your child's alphabet of life?

_____

_____

_____

_____

_____

_____

_____

_____

_____

_____

_____

_____

_____

A Space to Create

2 - TERRIBLE TWOS

These terrible twos were just as you might expect, full of emotion. One minute you are happy, and the next minute the world is ending. When you are two, you are still forming your words and trying to piece together the things you have downloaded from the people around you. In that same fashion, during this period in my life I did not know how to express myself as an adult. There were days of happiness, sadness, confusion, and unknowns. These were days that I wanted to do the impossible. I wanted to be able to rid myself of all pain with a snap. I wanted to set fire to the rain in my life. This chapter of my life is pure expression of trying to do the impossible on my quest to find my voice.

As the water flows down from my source of pain

As my heart beats faster than a runaway train

As my throat gets dry, and my soul feel slain

I search for gasoline to singe my pain

The smoke starts to rise, and the fire gets hot

My eyes are blurry, and my courage is shot

I just want to be happy and free from this pain

I close my eyes, open my lighter and

Set Fire to the Rain

Reflection

Pause and take a breath. Reflect to a time where you were on a quest to find something, whether it be your voice, healing, inner peace, etc. How did you navigate your journey? Journal about the quest you were on. While journaling, let yourself experience the feelings that led you to where you are today. Honor the things, good or bad, that you overcame and shaped who you are today. No matter what step you are on in your quest, YOU are doing great!

_____

_____

_____

_____

_____

_____

_____

_____

_____

_____

_____

_____

A Space to Create

3 - TRIUMPHS

I like to call this chapter of my life Triumphs because during this time, I experienced bullying, depression, and feelings of loneliness, but was still able to find my way out of these dark times. I wrote this poem when I started to love the skin I am in and love myself overall. Growing up, I realized I had issues with self-love. My issues weren't completely about my skin color, but more about how life continued to knock me down. I grew up during a time where "zero-tolerance" for bullying did not exist. Alternatively, I was met with the phrases "suck it up" and "what happens here stays here". This taught me to stuff my feelings and left me feeling like not many people cared. However, through maturation, I learned that life comes with scars, but all scars tell a story. This is my story of finding beauty in the scars.

My Black is Beautiful,
I was built Ford tough...
I got scars that run from head to toe, but never will I give up...
No, my story it ain't pretty, its full of grime and shade, but will I tell it?
Yea I'll tell it, with pride head held high...
no shame...my failure is my fame!
I fell...I got up...to be honest I stayed down a few times...
Did I cry...hell yea I did, inside I wanted to die...
But I was built Ford tough... I was built better you see...
Hurricanes, tornadoes, heartaches...they tremble at my feet...
I was built to be strong...not built to break,
But fight through adversity and swim through the pain...
My Black is Beautiful and so are the scars...
My story and scars though they ain't pretty, they tell the story of it all.

Reflection

Tell the story of your first triumph. Think back, really dig deep in the arsenal of your mind. When was that first moment you pulled yourself out the mud and guck? Whether it was from the trials of life, marriage, work, kids, etc. It doesn't matter if you made baby steps or took giant leaps, write about that moment you said, I did it! Celebrate yourself, don't be afraid to toot your own horn. TOOT TOOT!!!

_____

_____

_____

_____

_____

_____

_____

_____

_____

_____

_____

_____

_____

A Space to Create

4 - QUADRATIC COMPLICATION

Quadratic Complications as a title seems intense. Like, if it were a name of a math problem, you'd probably want to avoid it. My quadratic complication was my voice. I was taught manners, discipline, to respect my elders, etc. The complications came when I realized everyone wasn't taught the same things that I was taught. Everyone didn't have manners, respect, discipline, couth, etc. To be honest, if you caught me on most days, you'd think I wasn't taught these things either. My mouth was a sword and would cut you if you got too close. But, one day I went mute and stayed that way for a while. Writing and tears were my only outlet to say the things my mouth couldn't speak.

They see me when I'm smiling
But not when I hit the floor
They don't see me when I'm broken
Or even when I'm torn

They don't see me on the driveway
face red... crying for hours
They don't see me cradled deeply
In a bosom with no power

No power to raise my head high
No power to say a word
No words to say or mutter
For my soul has been disturbed

The pain has grasped my vocal cords
I cannot shout or scream
But my eyes are no one's captive
And with my tears they bleed.

Bleeding for the times I put a band-aid on a wound
Bleeding for the life hidden, captive in a tomb

21

Bleeding for the blood my hands wished they could claim
Bleeding from the cross that took away my shame

So, you may never see me broken
For only few do
I've cried and wept in silence
No longer shall I be mute.

Reflection

In life sometimes, there may be an event or situation that causes you to feel powerless. Have you ever been in a situation where you felt like you had no voice? Think back to where it happened; was it at work, home, a restaurant? Who muted you and how long did you stay silent? Have you shared with someone what it feels like to be voiceless? After writing, I encourage you to find a trusted individual and just use your voice. Also, I want you to listen to others. Make sure you aren't allowing your pain to be projected on to someone else and muting other people.

_____

_____

_____

_____

_____

_____

_____

_____

_____

_____

_____

_____

_____

_____

_____

_____

_____

_____

_____

_____

_____

_____

_____

_____

_____

_____

_____

_____

_____

P. Wolliston

A Space to Create

5 - CINCO MINUTOS DE MUERTE

Cinco Minutos de Muerte (Five Minutes of Death) is probably the most intense chapter of my life. This chapter addresses the trauma of when a trusted individual violated my trust and my innocence. The first violation of my innocence felt like Five Minutes of Death. I remember sounds, smells, and colors. I still feel sick when I come across specific smells. When I was violated, I remember hearing my own heartbeat disappear. Even now as I write, I remember more than I wish I did. Some people try to point the blame to me, but in my healing process I'm learning that most people have their own trauma lens that they see things through.

See you thought I was Down to Fornicate
Down to replicate...
Your plan was to eviscerate
To Deprive the Fullness thereof
You Denigrated the Facts
told a story that sounded good
But truth it lacked.

Damaged...
you Damaged the Flower you were supposed to water.
Triggered...
the gun you were meant to alter.
Forged...
a signature on sacred land.

You...
Disintegrated the foundation
Disillusioned the followers
Discounted the fertilizer meant to grow everything you crapped on.

I've...

P. Wolliston

Destroyed the Fears
Died to Flesh and
Decided to Forgive
I'm on a journey...
Be Blessed.

Reflection

No real prompt here. Just write what comes up. Reflect on any unhealed trauma and take steps to find the path to your own healing and love.

_____

_____

_____

_____

_____

_____

_____

_____

_____

_____

_____

_____

_____

_____

_____

A Space to Create

6 - RECOVERY

Anytime there is a recovery, there must be an acceptance that something had to be recovered from. You are halfway through these chapters of my life. For me, I was recovering from pain and hurt. However, through my recovery, I made a discovery. I am more than what meets the eye, more than pain and trauma. We all are. I wrote this poem during black history month in 2020 to celebrate those who look like me. This provided me with the feeling of pride and love and helped me to discover who I was.

I am 365
On blood moons, eclipsed suns
Not only the days you choose to see
My black always resides,
I am her and she is me

I am 365
My loc crown frames my face
My skin reflects the sun...
We began the human race

I am 365
Sometimes 366 on years like these
I leap through the years
As proud as my ancestors who descended from kings and queens

I am 365
This month cannot contain me
Like those chains tried to restrain me
Like the oppressors who detained me
I am exuding effervescence,
Diamonds dripping from my home

What kinda crap is this??
Ancestry asking me to pay them to tell me where I was stolen from.

Humph...
I am 365
I am the Mother Land
Uprooted and scattered on Mother Earth
Like a tree, neglected after being planted
I twist my roots deeper... for I shall not be moved

I am 365
I'm blackity blackity black
My colloquialisms coagulate
I code switch when I please
I say How are you doing this fine morning? When I feel out of place
I nod my head and say wessup when my soul feels safe

I am all that is and all that ain't
I am Doctor, Lawyer, Engineer, Author, and Astronaut
I'm not the things you think I am
I'm all the things you think I'm not

I am four fingers curled covered by one thumb

Screaming, One for all, and all for one
We are together in this sitch

I am...
We are...
365, sometimes 366

Reflection

Affirm yourself. Who are you? That is it! I will start you off... I AM...

_____

_____

_____

_____

_____

_____

_____

_____

_____

_____

_____

_____

_____

_____

_____

_____

_____

_____

_____

_____

_____

_____

_____

_____

_____

_____

_____

_____

_____

_____

_____

_____

_____

_____

P. Wolliston

A SPACE TO CREATE

7 - COMPLETE HONESTY

They say 7 is the number of completion, so I want to be completely honest. The truth is, I am flawed. I try to be a good person and do things the right way but sometimes, I don't. I can be rude, crass, insensitive, callus, and neglectful. As a Christian, sometimes people have an expectation that you are perfect. Sometimes, we are met with but, "aren't you a Christian?". My answer to that is yes, I am, but I am also a human who experiences highs and lows. I am a human who understands that I need to be real with where I am, so that I know what to work on to get where I need to be. My continuous effort is to be my best self. Some of you may know the Lord's prayer, but I had to be honest and write it exactly how I feel it. Welcome to my complete honest version of the Lord's Prayer.

Our Father who art in heaven...
My, I really need you here, because my heart is heavy ladened & my eyes are filled with tears
Hallowed be thy name...
I'm feeling weak, it's hard to speak, somethings gotta give Lord I'm feeling the strain of defeat.
Thy Kingdom come...
I'm ready Lord, how much longer is this pain...My inner beast provides no peace and I'm not Able to fight my Cain
Thy will be done...
But please Lord let your will provide me solace...I'm not sure I feel secure...I'm a wretch and unpolished
On earth as it is in heaven...
Am I in the right place, cause this place God it's destitute and should be looked upon with disgrace
Give us this day our daily bread...
Though I prefer the night, people can see through my shattered heart with the tiniest of light
And forgive us our debts...

LORD, I'm really in the hole, my life has lost its value... so please protect my soul
As we forgive our debtors...
I forgive it Lord I do, but I need your help... can you tell my collectors that this is what you expect from them too?
Lead us not to temptation...
I seem to find it on my own, please dim all these other lights so I see you alone
But deliver us from evil...
Ahh just what I need...I'm tired of this feeling I give it to you with ease
For Thine is the Kingdom, the Power, and the Glory...
I get it...its apparent why there is no one like you...I'm not worthy of your presence but I'm here to use if you choose.
Forever and ever, Amen.
Thank you, Lord forgive me, my life is lifeless without you.

Reflection

Be completely honest, where are you RIGHT NOW? I don't mean your physical location but where are you mentally, emotionally, or spiritually? You don't have to recreate the Lord's prayer, but on these lines, be transparent with where you are right now. Nothing is off the table. Write wherever you are. There is no judgement here. Be free, be authentic.

_____

_____

_____

_____

_____

_____

_____

_____

_____

_____

_____

_____

P. Wolliston

A Space to Create

P. Wolliston

8 - ENR8GED

I became "woke" later in life. But once you have been awakened you cannot be sleep again. You can try, but even when your eyelids close, you can still see. I don't think I woke up until I was 23 years old. I did not get it. I would hear words like disproportionate, disenfranchised, and have no idea what they meant. To some people, skin color is like your ticket to a concert. Do you have floor seat skin, nose-bleed skin, or general admission skin? Your epidermis determines the quality of life, treatment, and education you should receive. I hope you receive this poem with love and see that skin color is beautiful in the many shades it comes in, and not as a social and economic level.

Hands up, Don't Shoot!
Is the cry of my people
Guns drawn, eyes up
Searching for the church steeple

My God, is this my end
At the hands of a man
but at least I lose my life
At the hands of an enemy than a friend

My people without knowledge
We will perish.
So, we must band together
To avoid meeting our peril.

The skin that I was born with
Is the cause of much hate.
Slurs and disgusting looks
Because of my race.

If I could choose my skin color

41

I would choose it just the same
Because scars tell the story
And triumphs come with pain.
I would rather be oppressed than be
An oppressor...because like a Phoenix, I rise.
And once you reach the top, it matters not how hard the climb.

My people keep your head up
In this time of pain
Through the trials and the storm
Our freedom we will gain.

March on my brothers and sisters
Let our blood not shed in vain
Let our anger fuel our hearts
And not progress to rage.

Mike Brown and Trayvon Martin
And my other fallen ones
Your death will not be forgotten
Through our fight you still live on.

Reflection

Examine yourself. Whether you are Black, White, Asian, Latino/Latina, Native American, Pacific Islander, Caribbean, etc., we all play a role in making the world a better place. What are you doing to make change? Really think, what are you actively doing to create change for those who are disenfranchised and experiencing things at a disproportionate rate. Do you only think about what benefits you? Be real with yourself; this is your time to reflect and be completely honest. If you have some changes to make, write them down and set a date for when you are going to start. Tell someone and let them hold you accountable. You are going to do great!

_____

_____

_____

_____

_____

_____

_____

_____

_____

_____

_____

_____

_____

P. Wolliston

A Space to Create

9 - COVID **9**TEEN

COVID-19, something like a nightmare, and something like a dream.

COVID-19, what A dream, right?
Wrong as the song singing Land of the Free
While children going hungry having to steal to eat
Wrong as people still living in poverty
While people losing jobs due to "economy"

COVID-19, what A dream, right?
$1800 reasons, what a sacrifice
Guess cause I got candles, I don't need lights
I got little mouths to feed, guess I won't eat tonight

COVID-19, what A dream, right?
People dispersed
Nowhere to turn when it hurts
Covid diet
Loots and Riots
The violent asking for nonviolence

COVID-19, what A dream, right?
I mean, come on, I gotta be dreaming right?
I want to hug my mom, and squeeze real tight

Social distance
Health conditions
Politicians politicking

Vaccine? No vaccine?
Schools closed or opening?

COVID-19, what A dream, right?
If I close my eyes tight, I can see the light

I can see the plane pulling in for my next flight
Funny how COVID-19 pushed me to write.

COVID-19, what A dream, right?

Reflection

Phew, 2020 was no joke! While you reflect, I want you to think about what COVID-19 took from you. This may be a hard to think about, depending on what traumatic events took place. I want to push you to find peace in this situation. Even through this difficult time, was there something that COVID-19, or the previous month or year taught you or pushed you to do? For me, I never thought I would publish my life for the world to see. If COVID-19 or the previous years didn't inspire anything for you, write down the things you've always wanted to do but have been too afraid/busy to try. Write it down and set a date to start. No rushed timeline, just a start date. I believe in you!

_____

_____

_____

_____

_____

_____

_____

_____

_____

_____

_____

_____

A Space to Create

10 - AtTENtion

COVID-19 came in and shut the world down quick. On that fateful day in March the powers that be said, "the world is closed". There was no time to prepare. The pandemic forced isolations and gave everyone a glimpse of what it is like to be apart from one another. People we hadn't spoken to for years, now are the people we want to speak to. Children were forced to learn virtually. Families that were knit together had to be torn apart to protect each other. The elderly had to be shut in with limited visitors for their health. Personally, I took for granted that I had time, not just with my elders, but with everyone. My charge to you is to spend time with your loved ones, mend any broken bonds, and take advantage of the time you have now.

Shoppers,
Can I get your attention please?
The world will be closing in 15 minutes

15 minutes feels like seconds
I got 15 things to say
Granny please don't go
I'll give you 15 reasons to stay

Shoppers can I get your attention please?
The world will be closing in 10
10 minutes is not sufficient
I took for granted that you had time
I didn't give you my attention
Now, I'm trying to say goodbye

Shoppers can I get your attention please?
The world will be closing in 5
A pandemic struck, the dementia took
What I thought you'd leave behind

Can I get your attention please?
The world is now closed
You can't get back the time you lacked
But this is what you chose

Pay attention to those saying
Can I get your attention please?
Look how easily 2020 took us to our knees

Give the extra hug
Say I love you extra loud
Attend all the events
Let your family know you're proud

Can I get your attention PLEASE?
Because the Zoom funeral just won't do
When time is up
You won't be able to fix
The things you didn't say or do.

Reflection

Who do you need to give more or less of your attention to? Think about the people you missed spending time with during the pandemic. Who do you miss now? Think about the people you gave more of your attention to because of the pandemic. For those with families was it an unexpected blessing or nightmare to have to spend more time with your children, spouse, parents, etc.? For those living solo, was it a new experience spending more time with yourself? Don't focus on what the next problem is or will be. Focus on what you need to give more or less attention to. Hold yourself accountable and write below what changes you are going to make.

_____

_____

_____

_____

_____

_____

_____

_____

_____

_____

_____

_____

_____

_____

P. Wolliston

A Space to Create

11 - BEG1NN1NGS

Every year is a season of starting fresh. On 2020's New Year's Eve as I was writing, I began to think about how bad 2020 started off. I was working multiple jobs, days, nights, and weekends. I lived in a nice apartment but due to COVID it was lonely. Everything closed and so did my spirit. Nothing excited me, there were no more outside dates, and no more interactions. It was a breeding ground for depression. However, during this solitude, I learned a few new things. I taught myself how to play piano, learned how to make southern cornbread and macaroni and cheese. By the end of 2020, I started a business, and you are reading yet another manifestation of 2020. As 2021 began, a new life was beginning for me too.

I'm writing this on New Year's Eve
Because what better time to start something new
Than on a new year or a new day coming soon to a country
near you.

It's never too late to start,
it's only hard to begin
But you can crawl before you walk,
like we teach our children

I've been thinking am I good enough,
and maybe you have too
But fear breeds complacency
Faith will guide you through

Sometimes we lose sight of our own forests
Staying focused on one tree
Losing sight that we are here
no matter who sees

If you win and no one sees it

It doesn't mean you didn't win
If you fall in front of everyone
You can still get up again

No matter if we win in silence or followed by a brigade.
You matter, you can do this...
Be your own parade!

Reflection

What will you begin this year? Some people do New Year's Resolutions, so if you want, you can think of this exercise as that. Or, you can just write what this season will bring forth for you. How can you be your own parade? In the COVID 9 TEEN chapter you wrote some things you were too afraid/busy to try. Have you worked on any of those things you listed? If you have, write what you have accomplished just as a celebratory moment for your progress. If you have not, write one thing that you can do today to get started. Come back to this page in one week and update yourself on your progress.

P. Wolliston

A Space to Create

12 - 12 GAUGE

Just as a gun shoots forth ammo, experiences of life can shoot things out of you. It all depends on what type of vessel you are, what you put in, and what you take out. I hope throughout this experience you have been able to start/continue the process of your healing or journey. This poem is the close of the part of my life full of insecurities, and uncertainty, and the door to prosperity and growth. No matter what comes my way, I believe, I am where I'm meant to be.

Can you see me?
I'm where I'm meant to be
In isolation I found inspiration on who I aspire to be
On the 8th day I met disaster
On the 7th day I met you

And all my calculations brought no reparations
Nor reformations alluded to

The fire exploded inside me
Love was the firing pin
And what was exposed
Was only what was already built within

The guts it took to push myself
The tears that helped me swim
The heart that pumped out all my love
Is now spilled within.

These pages are my body
It is my masterpiece
One shot is all it took
to bring out the best of me.

Reflection

What are you made of? Take inventory of what characteristics make up your human vessel. Are you full of love, patience, kindness, and gentleness, or are you full of bitterness, resentment, anger, and judgment? After taking inventory, if you have any negatives, write a plan on how you will push yourself to work on improving. Make sure that you are feeding that which you want to grow. If you are feeding into love, love will grow, if you are feeding in to hate, it will do the same. Trials will come, but when they do, you have a choice to either give in to despair or bring forth what is already inside you.

_____

_____

_____

_____

_____

_____

_____

_____

_____

_____

_____

_____

A Space to Create

ACKNOWLEDGEMENTS

Thank you and congratulations for beginning your healing journey with me. I would like to acknowledge the people who were essential in bringing this book to fruition. To my husband Anthony, thank you for being patient during the days that were high and especially for the days that were low. To my sister Roxane, thank you for harassing me nonstop to be my most authentic self, and not allow anyone to stop me from speaking my truth. An additional acknowledgment to all my siblings for just being supportive of me in all my endeavors. To my publisher, Robin for being patient, honest, and compassionate. Lastly, I would like to thank my parents, for without you, I would not be here. I appreciate you both for the different roles you've played in my life which inadvertently helped to tell many parts of the 12 Chapters of My Life.